First Facts®

PRO WRESTLING SUPERSTARS

SHEAMUS
PRO WRESTLING SUPERSTAR

by Brenda Haugen

Consultant: Mike Johnson, writer
PWInsider.com

CAPSTONE PRESS
a capstone imprint

First Facts are published by Capstone Press,
1710 Roe Crest Drive, North Mankato, Minnesota 56003
www.capstonepub.com

Library of Congress Cataloging-in-Publication Data
Haugen, Brenda.
Sheamus : pro wrestling superstar / by Brenda Haugen.
pages cm. — (First facts. Pro wrestling superstars.)
Includes bibliographical references and index.
Summary: "Introduces readers to pro wrestler Sheamus:, including his gimmick and
accomplishments in the ring"— Provided by publisher.
ISBN 978-1-4765-4209-6 (library binding)
ISBN 978-1-4765-6003-8 (ebook pdf)
1. Sheamus, 1978—Juvenile literature. 2. Wrestlers—United States—Biography—Juvenile literature.
I. Title.
GV1196.S54H38 2014
796.812092—dc23 [B]   2013032495

Editorial Credits
Mandy Robbins, editor; Ted Williams, designer; Jo Miller, photo researcher; Jennifer Walker,
production specialist

Photo Credits
Corbis: Xinhua Press/Du Jian, 6; Getty Images for WWE: Michael N. Todaro, 5; Getty Images:
Bongarts/Joern Pollex, 13; Newscom: WENN Photos, 9, 14, 18, 20, ZUMA Press/Matt Roberts,
cover, ZUMA Press/Panoramic, 17, ZUMA Press/Steven Paston, 10

Design Elements
Shutterstock: i3alda, locote, optimarc

Printed in the United States of America in North Mankato, Minnesota.
092013   007771CGS14X
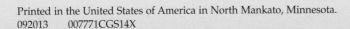

TABLE OF CONTENTS

A Tough Fight

June 28, 2013, marked the first Dublin Street Fight in World Wrestling Entertainment (WWE) history. Sheamus and Damien Sandow faced off. During the battle, it looked like Sheamus might lose. He had been punched, kicked, and smashed into stairs. Sandow hit Sheamus in the back with a stick before covering him for the pin.

pin—when a wrestler is held firmly on his back for a certain length of time

Sheamus delivers a Brogue Kick to Daniel Bryan's head.

Sheamus managed to kick out of Sandow's grasp just in time. He slowly took control of the match. Sheamus ended the fight with his famous Brogue Kick. Sandow fell to the mat, and Sheamus got the pin.

SIGNATURE MOVES

Sheamus' signature moves include the Brogue Kick and the High Cross. During the Brogue Kick, Sheamus jumps in the air and kicks his opponent in the face. To do the High Cross, Sheamus lifts his opponent above his head. He puts his opponent's arms out to form a cross. Then he throws him forward onto the mat.

signature move—the move for which a wrestler is best known; this move also is called a finishing move

BECOMING AN ATHLETE

Sheamus was not always the muscular picture of fitness he is today. He was born Stephen Farrelly on January 28, 1978, in Ireland. Stephen grew up in Cabra, a suburb of Dublin, Ireland. As a child he was short and overweight. That sometimes made him the target of bullies.

NO BULLIES ALLOWED

Sheamus is part of the WWE's STAR Alliance. STAR stands for Show Tolerance And Respect. The program aims to stop bullying by teaching children how hurtful it is.

suburb—a town or village very close to a city

Sheamus poses with a young fan.

Sheamus' father, Martin, was an **amateur** bodybuilder. As a teen Sheamus worked out with his father. Sheamus also enjoyed watching professional wrestling with his father and grandfather.

Sheamus loved tough sports. He played **Gaelic football** and **rugby**. He played on the National College of Ireland's rugby team in college.

amateur—describes a sports league that athletes take part in for pleasure rather than for money

Gaelic football—a team sport that combines elements of football, soccer, and rugby that is popular in Ireland

rugby—a form of football played by two teams that kick, pass, and carry an oval ball

A DREAM COMES TRUE

After finishing college, Sheamus worked with computers and as a security guard. He even worked as a bodyguard, protecting several famous people. But he dreamed of being a pro wrestler.

Sheamus traveled to the United States in 2002 to chase his dream. He went to a pro wrestling school in Paulsboro, New Jersey, called the Monster Factory.

The Monster Factory prepared Sheamus for tough WWE matches, such as this one against Big Show in 2012.

Sheamus lifts Drew Galloway over his head in an Irish Whip Wrestling match.

Sheamus practiced what he learned in real matches. But he took a bad fall during one match and hurt his neck. It took nearly two years for the injury to heal. But Sheamus wouldn't give up on his dream. He joined Irish Whip Wrestling (IWW) in 2004. In 2005 he won the IWW International Heavyweight Championship twice.

Sheamus became a star in the United Kingdom. But he wanted to be a star in the WWE in the United States. In 2006 and 2007, he tried out for the WWE. His second tryout led to a **development contract**. Sheamus started out in a small WWE league called Florida Championship Wrestling. By October 2009, Sheamus had worked his way up to WWE's major RAW brand.

development contract—a deal in which a wrestler is paid to compete in a smaller league as a way to train for a bigger league like WWE

Sheamus is the first Irish-born wrestler to win a WWE Championship.

Sheamus faced off with John Cena on October 4, 2010.

In December 2009 Sheamus battled John Cena for the WWE Championship. When the table match began, Cena took control. He had Sheamus in a hold and was about to throw him through a table. But Sheamus freed himself and pushed Cena backward. Cena crashed through the table. Sheamus had won his first WWE Championship.

table match—a match in which the winner must put his opponent through a table

A FAN FAVORITE

Sheamus has had his ups and
downs since he began pro wrestling.
But whether he wins or loses,
Sheamus' fans cheer him on. And
he's happy to be living his dream.

TIMELINE

January 28, 1978 – Stephen Farrelly is born in Ireland.

April 2002 – Sheamus begins training at the Monster Factory.

May 2004 – Sheamus joins Irish Whip Wrestling.

November 2006 and April 2007 – Sheamus tries out for WWE.

September 18, 2008 – Sheamus wins the Florida Heavyweight Championship by defeating Jake Hager.

December 13, 2009 – Sheamus defeats John Cena to win the WWE Championship.

January 29, 2012 – Sheamus wins the *Royal Rumble*.

April 29, 2012 – Sheamus defeats Daniel Bryan to win the World Heavyweight Championship.

June 28, 2013 – Sheamus beats Damien Sandow in the first Dublin Street Fight.

GLOSSARY

amateur (AM-uh-chur)—describes a sports league that athletes take part in for pleasure rather than for money

development contract (duh-VEHL-up-ment KAHN-tract)—a deal in which a wrestler is paid to compete in a smaller league as a way to train for a bigger league like WWE

Gaelic football (GAY-lik FOOT-ball)—a team sport that combines elements of football, soccer, and rugby

pin (PIN)—when a wrestler is held firmly on his back for a certain length of time

rugby (RUG-bee)—a form of football played by two teams that kick, pass, and carry an oval ball

signature move (SIG-nuh-chur MOOV)—the move for which a wrestler is best known; also is called a finishing move

suburb (SUH-buhrb)—a town or village very close to a city

table match (TAY-buhl MACH)—a match in which the winner must put his opponent through a table

READ MORE

Aiwei, Daniel B. *John Cena: Pro Wrestling Superstar.* North Mankato, Minn.: Capstone Press, 2014.

Dinzeo, Paul. *Sheamus.* Pro Wrestling Champions. Minneapolis: Bellwether Media, Inc., 2012.

Walker, Robert. *Sheamus.* Superstars! New York: Crabtree Pub. Company, 2013.

INTERNET SITES

FactHound offers a safe, fun way to find Internet sites related to this book. All of the sites on FactHound have been researched by our staff.

Here's all you do:

Visit *www.facthound.com*

Type in this code: 9781476542096

Check out projects, games and lots more at
www.capstonekids.com

INDEX